A Message for Adele

Written & Illustrated by Leo Winstead

To the memory of Sister Adele Brise,
for having the courage to follow God.
--Leo

Not so long ago, a young woman from Belgium named Adele Brise settled with her family in a remote town in eastern Wisconsin. The family worked hard in their new home, but the land was rough and filled with danger at every turn. One mild autumn day, Adele tread the winding path leading from her family's farm to the grist mill a few miles away.

All of a sudden, Adele froze in her tracks as she spotted a woman clothed in white between two trees. Before she knew what to do, the woman had disappeared.

Adele watched for the woman after returning from the mill, but saw nothing. When she arrived home, she told her parents everything that had happened. "Was it a poor soul in need of prayers?" they wondered.

*T*he next Sunday, Adele, her sister and one of her neighbors were on their way to church a few miles from home. They came close to the spot where Adele had seen the lady in white and now she had returned. "Oh, there is that lady again." Adele said in a startled, frightened tone. The other women could see nothing. After a moment the lady disappeared again.

After mass, Adele went to confession and spoke with the priest about what she had seen. "If the lady is from heaven, no harm will come to you," he advised. "You must ask in God's name who it is and what they want. Above all, have courage."

$\mathcal{A}$dele and her companions started the journey home, and when they came upon the site, the lady was there!

"In God's name, who are you and what do you want of me?' asked Adele."
'I am the Queen of Heaven, who prays for the conversion of sinners, and I wish you to do the same. You received Holy Communion this morning, and that is well. But you must do more. Make a general confession, and offer Communion for the conversion of sinners. If they do not convert and do penance,my Son will be obliged to punish them'

'What more can I do, dear Lady?' asked Adele.

" 'Gather the children in this wild country and teach them what they should know for salvation'

" 'But how shall I teach them who know so little myself?' replied Adele.

" 'Teach them,' replied her radiant visitor, 'their catechism, how to sign themselves with the sign of the Cross, and how to approach the sacraments; that is what I wish you to do. Go and fear nothing. I will help you.' "

$\mathcal{A}$dele wasted no time, but made preparations to follow the lady's request. She had her father build a makeshift chapel on the site where the lady appeared so that others could come and pay homage to heaven's queen. She walked from home to home along the peninsula, offering to teach the children their catechism and admonishing sinners.

*B*efore long, Adele had raised enough money to start a convent for other women who wanted to share in her mission. They were called the "Sisters of Good Health" and worked with Adele to open a boarding school for the children whom they taught and cared for.

Quite often, Sister Adele and the others would beg for food from the local farmers. After putting the children to bed, the sisters would pray to the Blessed Virgin Mary for help and, to their delight, they would awaken to a basket of vegetables or fresh meat on their doorstep the following day.

Many people began to visit the chapel to ask Our Lady for help. One boy named Michael, had fallen from a barn and was left crippled. He was brought to the shrine three times by some local women. After the third visit, Michael could walk! "I'm cured!" he exclaimed as he skipped out of the chapel. Michael was not the only one, many other pilgrims were also cured.

*S*ome people in authority doubted that Sister Adele had seen the Blessed Virgin Mary. Bishop Melcher of the diocese of Green Bay went to investigate her claims. She was ready to obey the bishop's command to close the school and chapel and offered up the keys to both. He was so impressed by her sincerity and zeal, he reconsidered. "You may continue your mission," the bishop said as he handed the keys back. "The children need you," and he added, "we all need Our Lady's help."

Not long after, a great fire erupted to the south. It swept into the Bay settlement and threatened to burn the chapel and school to the ground. Inside the chapel, Sister Adele carried a statue of Mary as the children prayed for safety. All night long, the children prayed the rosary. A storm came up and drenched the chapel putting the fire completely out!

*S*ister Adele's trouble was far from over. One day, on her the way to Mass, Sister Adele fell from a wagon and was badly hurt. It was too hard for her to handle all of the tasks from that point on.

She asked a younger sister, Maggie Allard to assume the role of superior. "With Our Lady's help, I will do my best." she proclaimed.

*S*ister Adele faced many other hardships until the end, but always turned to the Blessed Virgin Mary in times of need. After she had died, she was laid to rest near the chapel. One of her friends, Sister Pauline wrote: "She was always charitable and obedient. Her work prospered, and she did a great deal of good…Dear Sister Adele, from your happy home above, remember us."

*O*ver the years, many pilgrims have come to pray at the shrine of Our Lady of Good Help. Every year, on the Feast of the Assumption, a statue of the Blessed Virgin Mary is led in procession around the chapel grounds to commemorate the deliverance of the people from the great Peshtigo fire of 1871. A reporter writing for the Appleton Post once commented "Here in this humble farm field, in the heat of the day, and despite the odor the slight breeze brings in from the dairy herds, there is more piety than in the grandest cathedral."

Epilogue

Visitors continue to travel to the shrine to acknowledge and to celebrate all of the gifts that have been granted through the Blessed Virgin Mary's intercession. On December 8th, 2010, the Feast of the Immaculate Conception, Bishop Ricken gave approval to the 1859 appearances by Our Lady. He stated that they "exhibit the substance of supernatural character and are considered worthy of belief." He also recognized the shrine of Our Lady of Good Help as an official Diocesan Shrine for the diocese of Green Bay. Moreover, it is the first officially recognized Marian apparition in the United States of America.

Ave Maria!

Prayer to Our Lady of Good Help

Hail Heaven's Queen,
you chose Sister Adele to pray for the conversion
of sinners and to instruct the young in all aspects of the Faith.
Pray that we too may have the same courage, strength,
and determination to proclaim the Gospel in the wilderness
of our daily lives. O Most Blessed Virgin, give us the help
and protection we need to carry out this mission that
we share in Christ's name. Amen.